Original title:
Laughter in the Laurel

Copyright © 2025 Creative Arts Management OÜ
All rights reserved.

Author: Lucas Harrington
ISBN HARDBACK: 978-1-80567-436-8
ISBN PAPERBACK: 978-1-80567-735-2

Glee Among the Greenery

In the garden where fun takes flight,
Colorful blooms spark joy in delight.
Butterflies dance in a playful chase,
As giggles echo in this vibrant space.

Bouncing bunnies hop with glee,
Chasing shadows, wild and free.
The sunbeams flicker, a merry sight,
Creating moments of sheer delight.

Secrets of the Soft Breeze

Whispers flutter through the tall trees,
Tickling petals with gentle ease.
A secret smile shared on the air,
With every breath, joy everywhere.

The wind winks softly, teasingly light,
Carrying giggles, pure delight.
Every rustle a playful tease,
As nature's chorus begins to please.

Tickled by the Tender Leaves

Leaves chuckle as they twist and sway,
In a joyful dance, they find their way.
The branches sway as if in jest,
Inviting all to join this fest.

Sunlight pours like laughter's glow,
Painting the ground with a soft flow.
As whispers of fun come to life,
Mirth ignites in joy and strife.

A Harmony of Whimsy and Wonder

Nuts and squirrels play a game,
Crafting chaos without any shame.
Each rustle brings a hidden joke,
In this playground where laughter's woke.

Clouds drift by in silly shapes,
Imitating fun with silly tapes.
Together we bask in nature's cheer,
Creating memories year after year.

The Elation of Elders and Youth Alike

In winding walks where giggles bloom,
Old tales twinkle, dispelling gloom.
Elders wink with a playful tease,
While youngsters plot their next big freeze.

A kite takes flight in the summer sky,
With woeful winds that pass it by.
Yet shrieks of joy erupt and cheer,
Echoing smiles, far and near.

The game is on, with bumps and falls,
As laughter dances off the walls.
Grandma joins, with a youthful spin,
And who knew folly could lead to win?

Beneath the shade of a grinning tree,
We find our hearts wild and free.
In every chuckle and cheeky gruff,
We learn the secret: life is tough, but fun!

A Clarion Call to Celebrate the Day

When morning breaks with coffee's scent,
A chorus sings, with time well spent.
Hats askew and socks that clash,
We raise a toast with joyful splash.

The cake stands tall, with frosting dreams,
As party hats look like moonbeams.
Old jokes linger as fingers point,
While laughter flies, the merriment's joint.

They dance like shadows beneath the sun,
In silly ways that make hearts run.
Twist and twirl, then trip and fall,
Our giggles echo, a merry call.

So gather 'round with cake and cheer,
No need for crowns or gold to wear.
For in each chuckle, we sing our praise,
To celebrate the best of days!

Echoes of Joyful Whispers

In a forest where giggles roam,
Tree trunks wear crowns of foam.
Squirrels spin tales with winks,
Bubbling streams join in with blinks.

Sunshine tickles the dappled ground,
Where every footstep brings a sound.
A dance of shadows in playful flight,
Echoes of joy, oh what a sight!

Serenade of Giggling Leaves

Leaves shimmy under a bubbling breeze,
Birds share jokes, as they tease.
With every flutter, a chuckle flows,
Nature's revelry, everyone knows.

Blossoms burst forth, a vibrant cheer,
A rainbow of colors, bright and clear.
Petals whisper secrets in the sun,
Under this canopy, joy's never done.

The Dance of Playful Spirits

Sprites leap among the twisting vines,
In their dance, the sunlight shines.
Each twirl releases a bubbling sound,
As whimsy swirls softly around.

Punchy raindrops join the spree,
Pitter-patter mirthfully.
With every jump, a giddy grin,
The forest holds the spirit within.

Chortling Among the Canopy

Branches sway with a friendly tease,
Whispers chuckle in the breeze.
A clamor of laughter rings so clear,
From playful ghosts that wander near.

Frogs croak comedies by the brook,
While owls gaze with a knowing look.
Each rustle and giggle, a joyful sound,
In this place, happiness is found.

The Bright Side of the Forest Path

On a path where shadows play,
Squirrels dance without delay.
Tickled leaves in gentle breeze,
Whispers of the forest tease.

Beneath a branch that's full of glee,
A rabbit hops, so wild and free.
With every twist, a grin appears,
A chorus of the woodland cheers.

Revelations of Radiance and Bliss

Sunlight filters through the trees,
As frogs engage in silly pleas.
Each moment bursts with joyful sound,
Where giggles bloom upon the ground.

A whimsy here, a chuckle there,
Nature's jesters, full of flair.
Bright blossoms wink from every side,
In this realm, pure joy does abide.

Merriment Amidst the Oak and Pine

Among the trunks, a jester rolls,
With acorns tossed and playful goals.
A breezy dance of pinecone smiles,
Where even clouds have silly styles.

The critters plot a merry spree,
With rustling leaves, they twirl with glee.
In every nook, there's laughter stored,
Nature's charm, forever adored.

The Kaleidoscope of Cheerful Days

Through the branches, sunlight beams,
Painting dreams in vibrant schemes.
Wildflowers giggle in a row,
As breezes hum, and fireflies glow.

A palette bright, where spirits soar,
In playful prances, hearts explore.
With every turn, new joy unfolds,
A tale of cheer, forever told.

Harbingers of Happiness in the Grove

Beneath the trees, the giggles flow,
Squirrels dance in a silly show.
Branches sway with a playful tease,
Whispers of joy in the gentle breeze.

The sun plays tricks with shadows cast,
Joking around, oh what a blast!
Every leaf seems to chuckle loud,
Nature's wit, a cheerful crowd.

Traces of Humor on the Breeze

A chuckle floats upon the air,
The flowers grin with vibrant flair.
Buzzy bees hum a silly tune,
While butterflies dance under the moon.

The brook burbles in playful jest,
Tickling rocks, it does its best.
Clouds drift by in whimsical shapes,
Creating stories like funny scrapes.

Chasing Shadows of Delight

In every corner, laughter hides,
As shadow puppets play on slides.
Sunbeams bounce with a friendly wink,
While daisies nod and giggle, I think.

The grass whispers secrets, oh so sly,
In the playground where dreams fly high.
Each corner holds a smile's embrace,
Inviting all to join the chase.

Puddles of Joy in the Woods

Raindrops splash like playful cheer,
Turning paths to laughter here.
Each puddle reflects a joyful grin,
The earth's delight is about to begin.

Frogs in boots leap with glee,
Bouncing jokes from tree to tree.
Wet leaves rustle with a secret tease,
Nature's humor sways with ease.

Mirth in the Whispering Woods

In the glade where giggles grow,
Squirrels dance, putting on a show.
The sunbeams twirl, a playful crew,
While shadows whisper jokes anew.

The breeze carries a hearty cheer,
Echoing laughter far and near.
Mushrooms chuckle, swaying bright,
In this realm of pure delight.

Frolicsome Tales Under the Branches

Tales unfold beneath the trees,
As breezes tease with gentle ease.
Frogs croak rhymes, a ribbiting song,
While the owls hoot, 'You can't go wrong!'

With every tickle of the leaves,
The woodland whispers, never grieves.
Acorns tumble, causing mirth,
In the heart of this joyous earth.

A Serenade of Smiles and Sighs

A melody so sweetly spun,
Crickets chirp; the night has fun.
Bats play tag in the velvet sky,
As fireflies twinkle, oh my, oh my!

Each rustle holds a secret joke,
While dandelions puff and choke.
The moon winks down, a grinning friend,
In this lullaby that never ends.

Joyful Rustles Above and Below

In the meadow, where daisies sway,
Buzzing bees join the merry fray.
Ladybugs race on blades of green,
Cheerful contests, a sight unseen.

Rabbits hop with giggly glee,
Chasing shadows, wild and free.
The heart of nature beats with jest,
In this realm, we find our best.

Heartfelt Revels of Ferns

In the glade where ferns do sway,
A jester dances night and day.
With silly hats and shoes so bright,
He spins and twirls, a gleeful sight.

The squirrels chuckle from afar,
As he bumps into a tree or car.
His giggles echo through the air,
A joyful tune without a care.

Frogs join in with a ribbit cheer,
As butterflies flutter, oh so near.
A merry band beneath the sun,
In playful antics, all is fun.

When twilight falls and stars appear,
The fireflies wink, the laughter clear.
With every joke and playful tease,
The heart feels light, the spirit frees.

Hush of Happiness in the Woods

In dappled light where shadows play,
A gnome tends to his charms today.
His garden hops with giggling bees,
And happy blooms dance in the breeze.

A raccoon juggles acorns round,
While the owls hoot a friendly sound.
The whispered trees hold secrets tight,
Of every jest that starts the night.

The brook sings softly to the rocks,
As rabbits share their silly socks.
In every nook, a chuckle grows,
Where happiness and nature flows.

Such hush of cheer beneath the leaves,
Where nature spins its joyful weaves.
With each soft rustle, hearts rejoice,
Amid the woods, we find our voice.

The Gift of Joyful Mornings

The rooster crows with a cheeky grin,
The dawn is bright, let giggles begin.
As sunbeams tickle sleepy eyes,
The world awakes in sweet surprise.

With pancakes stacked and syrup dripped,
A clumsy cat takes a playful trip.
The laughter bubbles, warm and free,
New moments bloom like flowers, you see.

While coffee spills and dog will chase,
A race around the merry space.
With every sip, the joy expands,
Together we make the silliest plans.

As shadows dance and roosters crow,
Each morning brings new tales to show.
In playful hearts, our spirits soar,
The gift of joy we can't ignore.

Cheery Echoes in the Haze

In a meadow drenched in morning mist,
A playful sprite with a twinkle kissed.
He juggles clouds and chases dreams,
With ripples of laughter, or so it seems.

The flowers sway, they nod and grin,
As silly tales begin to spin.
With whispered jokes that travel far,
Where sunshine joins the frolic star.

A butterfly dons a jaunty hat,
While a bumblebee hums this and that.
The echoes of joy brush the clear sky,
With giggles and grins as spirits fly.

In this haze of light and cheer,
Every moment sings, so dear.
With every step, the heart will dance,
In the joyful rhythm of chance.

Vibrant Smiles in Silent Trees

In green shadows, giggles peek,
Breezes whisper fun and cheek.
Squirrels chuckle, branches sway,
Nature's jesters lead the play.

Each rustle holds a joyful tease,
Sunbeams dance with playful ease.
Underneath the watchful boughs,
Happiness in leafy vows.

Mossy stones and ferny beds,
Where sweet humor lightly treads.
Bright-eyed deer with grins so wide,
In this realm, no gloom can bide.

Whispers echo, all around,
In this grove, pure fun is found.
Every nook a secret cheer,
In the woods, the joy is clear.

The Prankster's Glade

In a glade where shadows play,
Elves conspire to tease the day.
With flower crowns and painted toes,
They spring surprises, who knows?

Crickets tune their chortling song,
As playful spirits dance along.
With twinkling eyes and mischievous grins,
The forest whispers of silly sins.

A breeze that tickles every leaf,
Bears witness to this joyful grief.
Catching giggles in a weave,
In this space, they never leave.

Their laughter ticks like clockwork gears,
Creating memories through the years.
In this glade, there's endless cheer,
A world of fun, all gathered here.

Musical Mirth Beneath the Canopy

Beneath the arch of greenery,
Frogs croak tunes so cheerily.
Bugle flowers hum a tune,
As the sun departs to moon.

Lively rustles set the beat,
Every creature taps its feet.
Trees sway in rhythmic delight,
While shadows dance in fading light.

Mice with hats and tiny shoes,
Join the band, they cannot lose.
With petals fluttering like flags,
Every note that laughter drags.

Echoes bubble in the stream,
Joyous moments reign supreme.
In a world where fun's the law,
Music fills the air with awe.

Laughing Colors of the Forest

Bright blooms giggle, colors bright,
Spreading joy from morn to night.
Bouncing berries, plump and round,
Bring a smile to sight and sound.

A painted lady flutters by,
With giddy strides that catch the eye.
Bumbles buzz with silly hums,
As the forest softly drums.

Frolicsome ferns wave their grace,
Chasing shadows with a race.
Every hue a playful jest,
Where merry hearts can find their rest.

In nature's palette, laughter glows,
A symphony where happiness flows.
With every brush and every cheer,
The colors whisper fun is here.

Splashes of Sunshine and Smiles

Bright beams dance upon the grass,
Joyful whispers, time does pass.
Children chase with gleeful shouts,
Sun-kissed faces all about.

Pies that fly and frogs that sing,
Every moment's a silly fling.
Tickled toes and playful falls,
Life's a game, come one, come all.

Colors swirl in vibrant skies,
Happy hearts and brightened eyes.
With every bounce and every leap,
Sweet laughter blooms, a treasure to keep.

Underneath the big blue dome,
Together we'll forever roam.
In a world of smiles and cheer,
Let's make memories, year by year.

Hilarity in the Grove

Wobbling squirrels and chattering birds,
Nature sings the funniest words.
Bouncing bunnies hop with glee,
Giggles echo like a melody.

Twisted branches, ticklish leaves,
Whispers playfully tease and weave.
A monkey swings, a shout, a cheer,
Every mishap brings joy near.

Sunlight bursts through leafy crowns,
Painting smiles on playful frowns.
Woodland critters in silly games,
All around, nothing's the same.

In this grove, laughter grows,
Chasing clouds, where happiness flows.
Let's dance with shadows, jump and play,
In this joyous place, we'll stay.

Tickles from the Treetops

Breezes carry whispers high,
Feathered friends flit and fly.
Branches bow with playful grace,
In this wild and wondrous space.

Chirpy songs and rustling cheer,
Nature's giggles fill the air.
Sunlight teases, shadows tease,
Each surprise brings forth a breeze.

Dancing hearts beneath the leaves,
Chasing joy, the spirit believes.
Squirrels play, then take a leap,
While laughter stirs from roots so deep.

With each flutter and every sway,
The world feels light, come what may.
Underneath the leafy spree,
We're wrapped in joy, forever free.

Giggles Beneath the Boughs

Whimsical whispers in the shade,
Down below, where dreams are made.
Rolling hills and playful streams,
World of wonder, life in dreams.

Beneath the boughs, where secrets hide,
We share our joy, no need to bide.
A splash of fun, a twist, a turn,
In this haven, bright hearts burn.

Leaves that chatter, branches sway,
Creating laughter all the way.
Bubbles rise and tickle minds,
Every moment, joy unbinds.

Laughter echoes, sweet and clear,
In our hearts, we hold it dear.
Gather 'round, let spirits fly,
Underneath this boundless sky.

Melodies of Bliss Under the Leaves

In the shade where the sunbeam plays,
Giggles dance in whimsical ways.
Squirrels prance in their merry routine,
Tickling branches, oh, what a scene!

Jokes float softly on the warm breeze,
While chubby bunnies nibble with ease.
The flowers chuckle, their petals wide,
As busy bees take a joyful ride.

Children's laughter, a sweet refrain,
Echoing softly, again and again.
Under the laughter beneath the trees,
The world spins round with such joyful ease.

Each whisper of wind brings a new jest,
Nature's comedy, surely the best.
With each chuckle, the day takes flight,
A festival blooms in pure delight.

Festive Serenades of the Grove

In the grove where the shadows play,
Joyful tunes bob up and sway.
Leaves chuckle as they flit and twirl,
While the mischievous critters whirl.

A raccoon winks from behind a tree,
With a sprightly vibe, wild and free.
Bells of laughter ring through the air,
While daisies dance without a care.

Glimmers of fun in the golden light,
Every nook filled with sheer delight.
The whispering winds carry a tune,
A melody sung beneath the moon.

With friends by our sides, we poke and tease,
Finding humor in moments with ease.
A whimsical world where spirits thrive,
In the grove, joy feels alive.

Chimes of Cheer Amongst the Pines

Among the pines, where the breezes chime,
The spirit of joy makes its climb.
Crickets chirp in a silly beat,
As playful shadows sway on their feet.

Silly hats atop furry heads,
Where laughter's a language widely spreads.
Pinecones tumble with a rhythmic thud,
Creating chuckles as they hit the mud.

Sunlight dapples through branches high,
Filling our hearts and souls to the sky.
They tease the shadows in the warm glow,
Creating mischief wherever we go.

In the company of the tall green trees,
Joy and laughter dance on the breeze.
Among the pines, life's a grand show,
Filled with giggles wherever we go.

Jolly Footsteps on the Trail

Footsteps light on a winding path,
Sprinkling giggles that spark a laugh.
Sunshine tickles the nose and feet,
While frolicking friends skip to the beat.

Each turn of the trail hides a surprise,
From raucous tales to brightening skies.
Jests float on the cloud-like air,
Tickling toes, an unmatched affair.

A nimble fox with a cheeky grin,
Mischief-making as we begin.
With nature's humor at our sides,
Joy travels with us on giggly rides.

As twilight wraps the world in glee,
Jolly moments weave a tapestry.
With every step, the heart takes wing,
A trail of joy, forever in spring.

Bright Echoes of Serene Laughter

In the garden where shadows dance,
A jester twirls, a merry prance.
With every step, the petals sway,
As giggles bubble bright as day.

Chasing bees, they buzz along,
Tickled leaves hum a silly song.
The sun peeks in, a playful grin,
With every chuckle, skies grow thin.

Bouncing kids with cheeks ablaze,
Spinning round, in joyous phase.
The breeze joins in, a sudden tease,
Cracking jokes with fluttering leaves.

A parade of smiles, bright and grand,
Joyful echoes fill the land.
With every chuckle, hearts take flight,
In this realm of pure delight.

The Secret of Joy Adrift

Hidden laughs in rustling trees,
Whispers float on the gentle breeze.
Silly games begin to bloom,
In this space where giggles loom.

A painted sky, a canvas wide,
Where shadows skip and dreams collide.
Joyful creatures leap and play,
Finding bliss in light of day.

Tickled flowers nod in time,
Each petal sways, a playful rhyme.
The world spins in a jolly twirl,
Where merry moments start to swirl.

Nature's jesters laugh and cheer,
A symphony so sweet to hear.
In the hush, a spark ignites,
Unveiling joy in morning sights.

Whispers of Delight in the Foliage

Among the boughs, a secret spills,
With every rustle, laughter thrills.
Mischievous breezes stir the air,
As nature plays without a care.

The sun peeks forth, a cheeky tease,
Caressing leaves with gentle ease.
Joyful giggles paint the morn,
In this realm where smiles are born.

Butterflies flit with colors bright,
Their dances spark pure childlike light.
Every twig and every vine,
Cracks a joke while we align.

Underneath the wise old oak,
Hidden glee in every stroke.
A haven filled with mirth around,
Where playful whispers can be found.

Sprightly Echos in the Meadow

In the meadow, blooms arise,
Chasing clouds and sunny skies.
Giggles flee on golden wings,
As flowers bloom and joybird sings.

Fields of laughter, bright and free,
Ticklish grass beckons me.
Each soft step a comic chance,
Where every heart begins to dance.

A chorus of joy, a merry play,
Chasing shadows all the way.
Mirthful tales are spun with ease,
In the arms of whispering trees.

Underneath the vast, blue dome,
Here all creatures find their home.
With every giggle, the world seems new,
In this meadow where laughter grew.

The Spirit of Fun in the Thicket

In the shadows where giggles grow,
Twisting vines put on a show.
Bubbles burst from hidden nooks,
While the trees wear silly looks.

A squirrel skitters with a grin,
Chasing shadows on a whim.
Every leaf begins to dance,
As nature joins in on the chance.

Jokes are whispered, soft and low,
Underneath the moonlit glow.
Echoes spin through fragrant air,
Tickling hearts without a care.

Bursting forth with playful cheer,
Laughter blooms, the sound is clear.
Joyful spirits take their flight,
In this thicket, day turns night.

Swaying to Joyful Rhythms

Dancing shadows, merry feet,
Twirling to a lively beat.
Every branch gives a little shake,
As the world begins to wake.

Breezes carry whispers sweet,
Tickling flowers, a joyous treat.
Nature hums a playful tune,
Bouncing under the playful moon.

Chirps and chirrups fill the sky,
With a wink and a happy sigh.
Each beat's a giggle in disguise,
Painting smiles on every rise.

Spin your partner, round and round,
In this revelry unbound.
In the thicket, joy extends,
As the laughter never ends.

Elysium of Glee Under Twilight

In twilight's glow, the stars do wink,
Where moments hang and giggles think.
Fireflies dance in careless flight,
As shadows giggle, sparkling bright.

A chatter here, a chuckle there,
Echoes whisper through the air.
Moonbeams twirl, they'll weave and glide,
In this realm where fun can't hide.

Cupcakes frolic with frosting dreams,
Bubbles dance in playful themes.
The night is young, let laughter soar,
With every joke, a heart will roar.

Sprinkled laughter, a charming blend,
Elysium's joy shall never end.
Underneath the twinkling light,
All who wander, feel delight.

Laughing Blossoms in the Breeze

Petals tumble with a laugh,
Each twist and turn a happy path.
Joyous blossoms, bright display,
Tickling hearts along the way.

With every gust, a playful cheer,
The fragrant utopia draws near.
Nature's giggle sings so free,
As skies shimmer with glee.

Wandering bees join in the fun,
Buzzing merrily, one by one.
In the garden, smiles abound,
As the world spins round and round.

Laughter ripples like a stream,
In this paradise of dreams.
With every bloom, pure joy is sown,
In the breeze, we're never alone.

A Tangle of Cheerful Moments

In the garden, giggles sprout,
Tiny flowers dance about.
Bees buzzing with a silly tune,
Chasing shadows 'neath the moon.

Jumping jacks with butterflies,
Tickled grass below the skies.
Sunshine's bright and full of glee,
Every moment wild and free.

Jokes exchanged with every breeze,
Waving branches, laughing trees.
Jumping puddles on a whim,
Letting giggles rise and brim.

Join the fun, oh what a spree,
Life's a jest, come laugh with me!
As the clock ticks, spirits climb,
In this tangle, rhythm and rhyme.

Card of Joy in Nature's Play

A squirrel slips, then takes a fall,
With acorn hats that crown us all.
Chirping birds declare a joke,
In leafy bends, they dance and poke.

Rabbits in a wild chase run,
Twisting, turning, purest fun.
Hopping high from here to there,
Nature's tricks hang in the air.

The brook chuckles, water sings,
As sunshine wraps in playful wings.
Laughter weaves through every glade,
A vibrant, joyful serenade.

From flower's smile to willow's sigh,
Each moment whispers, oh, so sly!
On this card, we'll ink delight,
In nature's play, our hearts take flight.

Whispers of Joy Beneath the Trees

Softly spoken, whispers rise,
Underneath the verdant skies.
Branches sway with gentle grace,
Each chuckle finds a cozy place.

A fox leaps high, gives us a grin,
Nature's jesters pulling us in.
From tangled roots to fluttering leaves,
Every corner, wonder weaves.

Brooks babble in friendly chatter,
What a world, where joy's the matter!
Twisting trails that lead us near,
In the woods, the fun is clear.

Gather round, let spirits soar,
In every rustle, seek for more.
These whispers flow like a sweet tease,
Joy dances softly, beneath the trees.

Trills of Tittering Leaves

In the breeze, they dance and sway,
Whispering secrets of a sunny day.
Each rustling giggle, a hint of glee,
  Nature's chuckles, wild and free.

Glimmers of sunlight bounce around,
Painting smiles on the soft, green ground.
Branches wave in a playful jest,
Nature knows how to have the best.

Squirrels chase shadows in a race,
Cheeky antics, in their little space.
Every twig a stage for their jest,
In this world, they are truly blessed.

And as the day begins to fade,
The trees share tales of a fun parade.
With each rustle, another cheer,
In the woods, joy is always near.

Rapture in the Green Canopy

Breezes blow with a playful song,
Fluffy clouds drifting along.
Leaves giggle in a soft embrace,
Nature's humor sets the pace.

High above, the branches sway,
Joking with the light of day.
Every shadow cast in fun,
A game of hide, a race to run.

Picture a bird, wings spread wide,
Not a worry, just pure pride.
Chirping verses of silly tunes,
In harmony with bright, round moons.

At dusk, the laughter starts to fade,
Whispers linger, never weighed.
In this green, a spirit unfurled,
Joy is alive in this vibrant world.

Hidings of Joy Among the Roots

Under the canopy, secrets hide,
Where giggles of critters coincide.
Roots twist like a playful vine,
In the soil, smiles intertwine.

Beetles march in a merry line,
Stomping to the rhythm, feeling fine.
Each tiny step a comical scene,
Dancing shadows on grass so green.

Twirling round in the soft, damp earth,
Every critter knows its worth.
Buried joy in playful nooks,
Whispered tales in shady crooks.

As the sun dips low and the sky turns bright,
The evening brings a festive light.
In each crevice, laughter does bloom,
A jubilant spirit among the gloom.

Tickle of the Treetops

Up above, the branches sway,
Tickling clouds, come out to play.
Merry leaves that wiggle and shake,
In the breeze, they spill their stakes.

With each rustle, a playful sigh,
Breezes whisper, let worries fly.
Clouds chuckle in a fluffy dance,
Nature invites us to take a chance.

Cherries chuckle, ripe and round,
Giggling softly without a sound.
Each juicy bite a burst of cheer,
The sweetest moments linger near.

As night descends with a soft hue,
Stars twinkle, sharing laughter too.
In the treetops, joy takes flight,
In this world, everything feels right.

Sunlit Smirks Beneath Green Canopy

In dappled light, the shadows dance,
With playful winds, the leaves entrance.
Giggles bubble from below,
As sunbeam paths make faces glow.

Squirrels chase, their tails a swirl,
Each twist a laugh, a joyful whirl.
The chatter grows within the grove,
Where secrets shared delight the whole.

Flowers wink with colors bright,
While butterflies take their flight.
Every petal, a giggle's tease,
Where smiles abound, and hearts find ease.

Beneath the boughs, a merry sight,
With echoes ringing, pure delight.
In nature's heart, mirth finds a home,
In sunlit smiles, we freely roam.

A Tapestry of Happiness Woven

With threads of joy, the fabric spins,
Each stitch a tale, where laughter begins.
Colors splash in bright array,
As moments twirl in charming play.

A patch of giggles, a quilt so warm,
Laughter weaves through every form.
Fingers dance with playful grace,
Creating smiles in every space.

Jests and japes, the yarns combine,
In this tapestry, hearts align.
Woven tales of silliness,
In every fold, sweet happiness.

Beneath the trellis, joy abounds,
With softest whispers, laughter sounds.
A fabric rich with vibrant cheer,
Where love and fun forever steer.

Grins Beneath the Ancient Trees

In the arms of giants, secrets lie,
Leaves chuckle softly, reaching sky.
Beneath the boughs, where shadows play,
A world of giggles brightens the day.

Frolicsome birds sing high and clear,
Their chirps a song that draws us near.
Bunnies hop, with mischief in sight,
As laughter rings, pure and light.

Breezes carry a whispering jest,
While sunlit beams put smiles to the test.
Each rustle of leaves, a playful tease,
Awakens joy with effortless ease.

Beneath these giants, hearts expand,
In nature's grip, we take a stand.
With grins that stretch from ear to ear,
In ancient woods, the fun is clear.

Gleeful Outbursts in the Wild

In twilight's glow, the critters roam,
Making merry, far from home.
A chorus bursts—each shout and squeal,
Celebrating life with zest and zeal.

The crickets chirp, a lively tune,
While owls join in beneath the moon.
With gentle mounds of grassy cheer,
The wild is filled with joy sincere.

Eager paws and feathered flights,
Creating fun on starry nights.
Every rustle, every sound,
A tapestry of glee unbound.

As laughter swirls through every glade,
The wild erupts in joyful cascade.
With nature's stage set for the show,
In gleeful outbursts, spirits glow.

The Breath of Joyful Reflection

Amidst the gleam of morning light,
Whispers tickle the buds of spring.
With each giggle, shadows take flight,
Nature plays, and the heart will sing.

Breezes dance with cheerful tunes,
Bubbles of joy float through the air.
Even the daisies wear wide moons,
Grinning bright without a care.

Ripples laugh as they rush and sway,
Catch a glimmer, a wink of cheer.
In this moment, worries give way,
Joyful reflections, simple and clear.

Here we wander, hearts open wide,
Finding humor tucked in each crease.
In the laughter, we take in our stride,
A warm hush, a delightful peace.

Unraveled Smiles Near the Stream

Curly reeds bob in playful jest,
Silly frogs leap with flair anew.
The creek chuckles, a jolly guest,
Glimmers dance in a sparkling hue.

Pebbles giggle beneath the flow,
Sketching stories in crooked lines.
Mirthful echoes in the undertow,
Even the fish wear silly designs.

With two sticks, children stir the mud,
Creating castles with wide-eyed dreams.
Splashing droplets, a joyful flood,
Turned memories into gleeful themes.

Around the bend, tales intertwine,
Every whisper, a jest to unfold.
Together we sit, sipping sweet wine,
The moment, a story, forever told.

Essence of Exuberance Among the Pines

Beneath tall soughing trees we play,
Ticklish breezes invite a chase.
Whirling leaves in a light ballet,
Nature's touch adds a smile to our face.

Sunbeams peek through branches spread wide,
Dappled shadows in a frolicsome game.
Crisp laughter bounces; joy can't hide,
Every nook feels like home, not the same.

Squirrels partake in a nutty spree,
While chipmunks join with a cheeky cheer.
Here joy plays out with pure glee,
A sweet sanctuary, we hold dear.

As twilight wraps the world in gold,
Stories hum under the starlit dome.
We gather warmth, our hearts unfold,
In this grove, we've carved out our home.

The Velvet Laughter of Dappled Sunlight

Golden rays cascade like ribbons bright,
Playful shadows twirl in delight.
Each blossom giggles, starts a show,
With petals fluttering, stealing the glow.

Bumbling bees in a bright parade,
Buzzing tunes as they merrily glide.
Every creature, a role well-played,
Nature's joy cannot be denied.

As the stream nods with a knows-it-all wink,
The sun dips low, a curious thought.
With each chuckle at the thought to drink,
Life unfolds in the joys it brought.

Gathering echoes of a pretty song,
We chase the day 'til the stars take flight.
In velvet laughter where we all belong,
Joy resides in the softest light.

Elfin Giggles from the Underbrush

Tiny feet dance in the leaves,
With whispers of mischief that never deceives.
A twinkle of light and a sprinkle of glee,
A chorus of chuckles from roots to the tree.

The fairies play tricks on the curious knight,
With whoopee cushions they toss in the night.
A hat made of daisies, a grin ear to ear,
In the thicket, you'll find them, delightfully near.

Gnomes roam the glen with their poppyseed pies,
Tickling the ribs of the wisest of flies.
Addi-dum-dum! Let's join in their song,
With giggles that bounce where we all belong.

Laughter erupts like the bubbling brook,
From shimmering faces in each hidden nook.
As moonlight spills out and the shadows take flight,
The night becomes woven with joy and pure light.

The Soundtrack of Silly in the Bloom

A meadow of blooms painted colors so bright,
Where silliness reigns, every day, every night.
The bees wear funny hats, swaying with glee,
While butterflies tango with a hop and a spree.

The daisies erupt with a ticklish embrace,
As rabbits in bowties engage in a race.
Clouds turn to cotton candy, drifting on by,
With giggles of giggles echoing high.

The gopher pops up with a surprising flair,
Juggling the acorns and flinging them with care.
While the drums of the crickets keep time with the sun,
To a playful symphony—oh, isn't it fun?

As shadows grow long with the warm fading light,
The flowers join hands in a whimsical fight.
And in every petal, a chuckle you'll find,
A soundtrack of joy that forever is kind.

Fill of Silliness Among the Shrubs

Among the green arms of the cozy old shrubs,
Lurk critters who laugh as they gather their clubs.
A choir of chuckles erupts from below,
As a hedgehog does cartwheels, putting on a show.

Squirrels wear glasses, pretending to read,
Dancing around like they're planting the seed.
The bushes are swaying in jubilant haze,
While the butterflies flutter their whimsical ways.

A frog tells a joke with a wink and a grin,
As the others all chuckle, their laughter a din.
Rabbits try backflips, but tumble instead,
With squeals of delight as they roll on their head.

At dusk, when the stars twinkle bright overhead,
The merriment soars, all the worries are shed.
For nestled in foliage, with each playful glint,
Is an echo of joy that we all are a hint.

Cascade of Cheer in the Landscape

In valleys where giggles cascade down the hill,
Where echoes of happiness ring loud and shrill.
Sunshine spills laughter like petals in flight,
As the world dances round with the twinkling night.

The bunnies spin tops, the hedgehogs clap paws,
While the owl sways gently—oh, what a cause!
Each rustle of grass is a song of delight,
As nature revels on through the magical night.

With mirthful explosions of daisies and glee,
The brook babbles tales as it skips past the tree.
In hues of bright joy, every color is spun,
As the landscape ignites into merriment fun.

So gather the giggles and dance with the breeze,
Join the jovial chorus among the tall trees.
For in this free spirit of cheer and of play,
The cascade of joy forever will stay.

Echoes of Merriment in the Glade

In the glade where laughter sings,
Whispers of joy from playful things.
Breezes tickle the leaves above,
Nature's chorus, a song of love.

Squirrels prance with cheeky glee,
Chasing shadows, wild and free.
Bouncing around with a playful race,
Smiles scattered in every space.

The brook chuckles as it flows,
Tickled by the sun that glows.
Hopping frogs with a croaky cheer,
Each ripple dances, holding dear.

In this haven, bliss takes flight,
Echoes of joy, a pure delight.
Every giggle, a spark anew,
In the glade, the heart feels true.

Sunshine and Giggles Amidst the Foliage

Sunshine streams through leaves so bright,
Where giggles chase away the night.
Witty whispers travel round,
In this haven, fun is found.

Blossoms chuckle, and the branches sway,
As cheeky critters plan their play.
Fragrant blooms join in the jest,
Painting joy, nature's best.

Beneath the arch of shady green,
The world feels like a playful dream.
Frolicsome moments here abide,
With lightness as our joyful guide.

In forest hues, where laughter thrives,
Every heartbeat, joy derives.
Together dancing, wild and free,
In sunshine's glow, we're meant to be.

Chasing Shadows with a Smile

In the sun, shadows leap and prance,
  Playful spirits in a jovial dance.
With every twist, a cheeky grin,
  Life's a game, let's dive in.

The grass invites with a ticklish tease,
  As butterflies flutter on the breeze.
Swaying trees whisper silly tales,
  Of daring dreams and giddy trails.

Rabbits hop with a mischievous cheer,
  Creating laughter as they appear.
Every rustle, a chuckle shared,
  In this chase, who ever dared?

With shadows dancing, spirits high,
  We find joy beneath the sky.
Each moment kissed by the silly game,
  Chasing shadows, never the same.

The Dance of Lighthearted Spirits

In the woods where spirits play,
Lighthearted hearts spin through the day.
With every step, the ground vibrates,
A dance of joy, the world awaits.

Beneath the boughs, with giggles bright,
They twirl and spin in pure delight.
Crickets serenade with a tune,
As moonlight winks, a playful boon.

Joyful breezes lift them high,
As they whirl beneath the sky.
Every clumsy leap, a fun surprise,
With twinkles bright in their eyes.

In this frolic, worries flee,
With every moment, wild and free.
In the dance, we find our spark,
Lighthearted spirits, bright in the dark.

Revelry in Nature's Embrace

Beneath the trees, the squirrels play,
Chasing their tails in a merry ballet.
Breezes giggle through leaves so bright,
While flowers fashion hats in the light.

Frogs croak jokes by the shimmering pond,
Each croak a pun, the air particularly fond.
Birds whistle tunes that tickle the mind,
Nature's jesters, joyfully entwined.

Bumblebees buzz in a silly parade,
Dancing in circles, never afraid.
With playful nudges, the petals dance,
In this realm of cheer, we take a chance.

Sunlight sparkles like laughter spilled,
Every shadow's thick with the joy it build.
Under the canopy, the world seems bright,
In this embrace, the heart takes flight.

Jests of the Woodland Dwellers

Rabbits hop with a cheeky flair,
Playing hide and seek without a care.
The woodpecker's tap is a beat so grand,
While chipmunks frolic, a merry band.

Each rustling leaf holds a secret giggle,
A joke exchanged in a sprightly wiggle.
The ants march in lines, a silly parade,
Stomping their feet on a leaf-made glade.

Foxes grin with a glint in their eyes,
Their antics a show full of surprise.
As shadows dance in the glowing sun,
The forest chuckles, its heart full of fun.

In the twilight's glow, the hoot of an owl,
Whispers a riddle, a cosmic prowl.
Nature's revelry, a song that swells,
In every nook, the laughter dwells.

The Sound of Chuckles in the Canopy

The branches sway with a playful cheer,
Echoing jokes that only we hear.
In this high realm, the sun shines through,
Sending giggles on a light breeze, too.

A parrot shouts with a twist of a word,
Making us laugh at the truth absurd.
The squirrels exchange their nutty tales,
While rabbits plot in the moonlit trails.

Underneath stars, the whispers resound,
As fireflies twinkle, a luminous crowd.
The night carries on with a soft, bright grin,
In the canopy's embrace, we all fit in.

With each rustle and clap, the joy we share,
Is woven in nature beyond compare.
Among the leaves, laughter takes flight,
In a realm of delight, from morning to night.

Radiant Moments in the Arboreal Realm

In the heart of green, the sunbeams laugh,
Sprinkling joy like a warm, sweet bath.
Tree trunks giggle, their bark telling tales,
Of woodland pranks and mischievous gales.

The leaves whisper secrets in playful tones,
As shadows leap and dance on stones.
In this timeless space, the world feels light,
A festival hidden from harsh daylight.

Lizards parade with a charming flair,
Winking at insects without a care.
The breeze sings softly, a melodic tease,
As flowers sway in the gentle ease.

Each moment unfolds like a curious jest,
Nature's wonder, a jubilant fest.
In this arboreal realm, delight does bloom,
With every giggle, heartbreak finds room.

Whimsy Woven in Nature's Tapestry

In the breeze, a giggle floats,
Swaying branches, happy notes.
A squirrel dances through the trees,
Chasing shadows, playing tease.

Beneath a bloom, a bumblebee,
Buzzing tunes, so wild and free.
A rabbit leaps, a jaunty prance,
Nature's stage, the world astance.

The sun above, with warmth it beams,
And tickles petals, full of dreams.
A chipmunk with a cheeky grin,
In this mirth, we all begin.

Starlit night, with twinkling lights,
Makes the world feel just so right.
Each twirling leaf, a playful jest,
In this realm, we find our best.

Joy Unfurled on Gentle Leaves

On breezy days, the laughter sings,
With fluttering wings, the joy it brings.
A bouncing brook, with rippling cheer,
Whispers secrets only we hear.

Petals dance, as the wind does play,
Colorful smiles in bright array.
A ladybug, with spots for flair,
Turns a simple stroll to a fair.

In dappled light, shadows leap,
Where memories of giggles seep.
Tiny frogs in joyful croak,
Nature's jest, a friendly poke.

The world spins in a playful twirl,
As daisies wink in bold unfurl.
Joy gleams bright in the gentle leaves,
Each whisper soft, a heart that believes.

A Symphony of Smiles Beneath the Sky

Clouds roll in with giggly grace,
Painting the horizon, a cheerful face.
A butterfly flutters, soft and spry,
In this realm where joy can fly.

The sunshine breaks, a burst of fun,
Chasing shadows, everyone!
With each tickle of the breeze,
Nature's laugh, a sweet disease.

Silly squirrels in playful fights,
Chasing tails on sunny nights.
The grassy hill, a slide so steep,
A merry ride makes the heart leap.

A symphony of glee unfolds,
As nature's magic gently molds.
With each smile and flicker of wings,
Life's whimsical dance begins to sing.

Hearts Warming the Cosmic Space

Stars giggle down from skies above,
Sprinkling twinkles like endless love.
Planets pirouette with joyful glee,
While moonbeams shine on you and me.

Galaxies spin in a playful race,
Chasing comets in a whimsical chase.
The universe hums a merry tune,
Beneath the watchful eye of the moon.

Hearts connect in this vast embrace,
Each laughter echoing through the space.
Cosmic bubbles of joy expand,
Binding all with a light, friendly hand.

In every corner, whispers ignite,
Filling the cosmos with pure delight.
A dance of souls, a swirling place,
Together we find our quirky grace.

Joyous Currents Through the Woods

In the glade where shadows dance,
A squirrel dons a hat askew,
With acorns as his treasure trove,
He prances wildly, oh so true.

A rabbit hops in stylish shades,
And stops to show a little flair,
The trees all chuckle in the breeze,
With every twirl, they seem to care.

An owl with jokes that spin like tops,
Recites them to the passing deer,
They roll their eyes, then burst in giggles,
As twilight brings a night of cheer.

In this wood where fun ignites,
Each creature plays a merry game,
From chorus frogs to buzzing bees,
All join the antics, none the same.

Playful Pitter-Patter

Raindrops tap a jaunty beat,
As puddles muster up a cheer,
A fox in boots takes to the lanes,
 Spinning tales for all to hear.

The ducks parade in patterns grand,
Quacking jokes, they strut and sway,
 Each splash a burst of silly fun,
 Their feathery frolic on display.

Mushrooms giggle in their spots,
As piglets scurry 'neath the trees,
With each squelch, a chuckle's born,
 Echoing on the soft, damp breeze.

In this dance of sky and ground,
Joy bubbles up with every tease,
A world composed of playful hearts,
Where laughter weaves through vibrant leaves.

Whimsical Sway of the Branches

Branches lean with cheeky grins,
Swaying tales of yesterday,
A songbird, decked in vibrant hues,
Trills a tune that laughs away.

A gentle breeze, a twisty gust,
Tickles leaves in silly ways,
As crickets join the evening choir,
With chirps that spin in bright arrays.

The moon peeks in with a wink so sly,
The stars burst forth in playful glee,
Watching nature's bright parade,
Their sparkle mirroring the spree.

In this grove where mirth is king,
Life dances with unyielding class,
Each whisper twirls, each gesture sings,
A joyous reverie shall last.

Frolics in Nature's Embrace

Beneath the boughs, the critters sing,
With acrobats that leap and twirl,
A chipmunk teases, stealing hearts,
While fireflies weave in silky whirl.

The brook giggles with each splash,
Racing stones in wild delight,
While beavers build their wobbly dams,
To host a party every night.

With every rustle, joy takes flight,
As laughter ripples through the glen,
From deer to ducks, each life embraced,
In nature's arms, where fun begins.

Here mischief blooms in petals bright,
And every twist suffused with grace,
A world alive with play and jest,
In every nook, a smiling face.

Sparkling Joy Beneath Verdant Arches

In a grove where shadows play,
The whispers dance, they twist and sway.
A jester strolls with tricks to share,
And all around, giggles fill the air.

A squirrel leaps from branch to branch,
With acorns poised for a light-hearted prance.
Nature beams with a mischievous grin,
As children chase the breeze and spin.

Beneath the leaves, a voice rings clear,
A melody of joy that draws us near.
The sun peeks through in golden rays,
And hearts unleash their carefree ways.

With each echo of a playful jest,
We find our souls at playful rest.
In laughter's glow, we twirl and twine,
In vibrant hues, our spirits shine.

Playful Spirits in the Sun-Dappled Grove

Under blooms of rosy light,
The playful sprites take off in flight.
With echoes sweet and stories told,
The air is warm, the laughter bold.

A fox prances, tail held high,
With leaps that make the sparrows fly.
Each rustle in the emerald hay,
Brings giggles forth throughout the day.

Among the trees, the shadows play,
As whispers tease the leaves to sway.
The sun, a bright and cheeky friend,
Commands the heart to twist and bend.

So let the melody rise and shine,
Where playfulness and joy entwine.
In every nook where smiles collide,
Life blooms, and all our woes subside.

Harmony of Laughter in Nature's Heart

In gardens where the wildflowers dance,
Nature sings in a joyful trance.
Each petal sparkles, each leaf a cheer,
Inviting all to gather near.

With butterflies joining the happy thrum,
A bustling breeze plays a happy drum.
The brook below giggles and flows,
As sunshine wears its brightest clothes.

A rabbit hops, with mischief in stride,
Around it all, the world's alive.
In each chuckle, the trees respond,
With rustling leaves, a joyful bond.

Celebrate here, in this vibrant space,
All worries fade, none can replace.
For in this heart where joy is art,
We find the rhythm of every heartbeat's part.

The Festival of Light Beneath the Boughs

Underneath a sprawling tree,
A festival bursts with glee and spree.
The lanterns twinkle, stars collide,
As revelers come, with joy as their guide.

Each step is lively, each song a cheer,
Inviting all to draw near.
The jesters juggle, and faces gleam,
In this moment, we find our dream.

With friends and shadows dancing bright,
We celebrate the playful night.
With laughter ringing in every heart,
A melody where friendships start.

Beneath the moon, the world unspins,
In our hearts, the festival begins.
So gather round in joyous throngs,
For this is where we all belong.

Revels Amidst the Flora

In a garden where the giggles bloom,
Petals dance to a merry tune.
Bumblebees prance with silly flair,
While butterflies twirl without a care.

Sunlight spills like a joyful drink,
Colorful blooms wink and blink.
Nature chuckles in gentle breeze,
As daisies gossip with hidden tease.

Squirrels leap, a comical sight,
Chasing shadows, oh what a flight!
Dandelions puff with cheeky glee,
Sharing secrets with each honeybee.

In this realm of whimsy and cheer,
Every laugh invites more near.
Joyous echoes fill the air,
In the heart of nature's funny glare.

The Blissful Echo of Shadows

In the twilight when shadows creep,
Whispers of mirth begin to leap.
Amidst the trees, a soft chuckle plays,
As the stars ignite the night's ballet.

Crickets chirp a jovial song,
While fireflies dance, they can't go wrong.
The moon giggles, casting its glow,
Beneath its watch, the silliness grows.

A rustle reveals a playful breeze,
Tickling leaves with mischief and tease.
Every glimmer, a secret to share,
In the shadows, laughter hangs in the air.

Frogs croak jokes from the pond's bright rim,
While owls hoot with a whimsical whim.
This night of delight, nothing to dread,
As happiness whispers, just follow its thread.

A Canvas of Cheer Under the Oak

Beneath the oak, the world stands still,
A canvas where joy meets thrill.
Picnics set with laughter in tow,
As merry voices start to grow.

Kites soar high in vibrant hues,
Each swirl a story, a playful muse.
Children chase the wind's sweet song,
In this haven where hearts belong.

Ants march in lines, a comical parade,
While squirrels plot a nutty charade.
Under the branches, shadows play,
As giggles tumble and float away.

Raindrops tap with a cheerful beat,
As puddles form beneath happy feet.
In this quirky space, we all unite,
Creating memories with pure delight.

Hues of Happiness in Between the Valleys

In valleys deep where laughter resides,
Colors burst like joyous tides.
Each flower whispers a witty jest,
Inviting all to join the fest.

Hills roll like giggles, bright and round,
Playing hide and seek with the sound.
The sun peeks in, a playful grin,
Illuminating the joy within.

Streams babble with secrets untold,
As stones chuckle in warmth from the cold.
The breeze carries puns on its wings,
In this realm of wonder, laughter clings.

Painting moments in vibrant strokes,
Joy leaps forth in uncomplicated folk.
In valleys where happiness reigns supreme,
Each heartbeat echoes a playful dream.

Revelry of the Forest's Heart

In the woods where the critters play,
Squirrels dance in a cheery fray.
Rabbits hop in a silly race,
Tickling trees with a smiling face.

Birds burst forth in gleeful song,
Who knew woodland could be so strong?
Twigs a-twirl, they spin with pride,
Nature's jesters on every side.

Frogs leap high with a joyful croak,
Each splash sends ripples, a funny joke.
Leaves giggle as they flutter down,
In this green mirth, there's no such frown.

Moonlight peeks through the leafy veil,
Whispers of joy in the nightingale.
Every rustle brings a grinning cheer,
A celebration of all those here.

Chuckles in the Glade

In the glade where the sunlight beams,
Foxes prance and follow dreams.
A brook that gurgles tricks and fun,
Jest after jest, it's never done.

Butterflies hug the blooms so tight,
Wings aflutter, a colorful sight.
Bumblebees hum with a buzzing joke,
As daisies laugh beneath the oak.

Pinecones tumble like little balls,
A rolling contest, nature calls.
With every drop, a silly sound,
In this glade, pure joy is found.

Wildflowers sway with a gentle tease,
Whispering secrets to the breeze.
Underneath the trees, we play,
A lively world in bright array.

Mirthful Murmurs of the Wind

The wind whispers secrets through the trees,
Carrying giggles with every breeze.
Clouds meander in joyful lines,
Painting the sky with chuckling signs.

Rustling leaves join in the jest,
Nature's cheer, we feel so blessed.
A dash of humor flows through the air,
Tickling noses, a playful flair.

Dandelions puff in a playful cheer,
Sending wishes of joy far and near.
Each tiny seed on its merry flight,
A journey of chuckles into the night.

As branches sway and flowers twirl,
The woodland dances, life in a swirl.
With every rustle, a laugh so sweet,
Echoes of glee in nature's heartbeat.

Jesting Shadows on the Ground

Shadows stretch and start their play,
Twisting shapes in a light ballet.
Silly forms that bounce and glide,
Mimicking dances, oh what a ride!

Grasshoppers leap with a comic twist,
All in sync with the sun's bright mist.
Twirling around in circling fun,
Each shadow sways, never to run.

Treetops chuckle as they sway,
Casting giggles along the way.
Swaying back and forth like fools,
In this lively playground of golden pools.

The sun dips low, shadows grow long,
Still the air is rich with song.
In every giggle, we find delight,
A joyful dance until the night.

Moments of Mirth in the Clearing

In the shade where shadows play,
A squirrel juggles nuts all day.
The brook giggles, bubbling bright,
Tickling toads in pure delight.

The trees wear hats of leafy green,
Whispering secrets, oh so keen.
A rabbit dances, skipping high,
While butterflies laugh in the sky.

Mice wear shoes, the antics grand,
Chasing their tails, they make a stand.
The breeze sings tunes, they prance around,
Creating joy in the soft ground.

In every nook, a chuckle hides,
Nature's jest, where mirth abides.
Follow the sound, embrace the glee,
In this realm, we're wild and free.

Eternal Smirks of Nature's Palette

The daisies wink with golden rays,
As sunlight dances through the haze.
The wind chuckles, a playful blow,
Tickling petals, stealing the show.

A ladybug, on a leaf, turns round,
In polka dots, she spins and bounds.
While frogs in puddles wink their eyes,
Singing tunes to the bluest skies.

Mushrooms giggle under the night,
In moonlight's glow, they feel so bright.
The stars above twinkle in jest,
Nature's art in a lively quest.

Each hue and shade, a playful tease,
In the wild's embrace, we find our ease.
With every breath, a smile we share,
In this palette, joy fills the air.

Jests of Faeries in the Hollow

Beneath the boughs where whispers sigh,
Tiny sprites flit and fly.
With jeweled wings and mischief bright,
They tickle toes in the soft moonlight.

A gnome may trip with a chuckle loud,
While shadows dance in a playful crowd.
The old oak groans with a hearty laugh,
As faeries plot their silly craft.

In the hollow's heart, surprises wait,
Where giggles bounce and don't hesitate.
The fireflies twinkle, playing tag,
Their glowing laughs, a joyful brag.

A playful breeze brings tales anew,
Of mirthful games the faeries do.
Come join the fun, let worries cease,
In this hollow, find your peace.

Sunshine in the Secret Garden

In the secret patch where the daisies bloom,
The sunbeams giggle, dispelling gloom.
A cat with a hat, so sly and spry,
Pretends to chase the butterflies high.

The hedgehog rolls down a gentle hill,
With laughter echoing, it's quite a thrill.
While blooms whisper jokes in fragrant tones,
Creating cheer in petal phones.

A twirling breeze plays peek-a-boo,
And tulips nod, as if they knew.
With every rustle, joy plants its seed,
In this garden, hearts feel freed.

So hark the calls of sweet delight,
In this sunny space, oh what a sight!
Where nature's humor paints our day,
In a wonderland where we can play.

www.ingramcontent.com/pod-product-compliance
Lightning Source LLC
Chambersburg PA
CBHW051649160426
43209CB00004B/849